IF YOU **FULLY TRUST**
THE POLITICIANS WHO RUN YOUR COUNTRY
AND THE OWNERS OF YOUR BANK,
YOU DON'T NEED TO READ THIS BOOK.

Summary

Introduction
How to Identify the TOP of the crypto market…...................5

The 4 Phases of a Market Cycle
1. Accumulation Phase…...7
2. Mark-Up Phase…..8
3. Distribution Phase…...9
4. Mark-Down Phase..10

Crypto Money Flow Simplified..11
Altcoins Market Share...12

The Bitcoin Halving
What is Bitcoin Halving?...14
Basics of the Bitcoin Network..14
Basics of Bitcoin Mining..15

Bitcoin Halving Effects
Inflation..17
Investing...17
Demand..18
Mining..18
Consumers..19
What Happens When Bitcoin Halves?..................................19
What Happens When There Are No More Bitcoins Left?......19
The Bottom Line..20

Summary

Crypto Indicators
Social Sentiment Indicators...22
On-chain metrics..24
On-chain metrics - MRVR Z-Score.....................................25

On-Chain Analysis: An In-Depth Look
1. What is On-Chain Analysis...26
2. Definition and Context..27
3. The On-Chain Analysis difference..................................27

On-Chain Analysis: Tools and resources
1. Understanding the origin of data....................................28
2. Identifying patterns and insights.....................................28

Five On-Chain Indicators
1. Stock-to-Flow (S2F)...30
2. Stablecoin Supply Ratio (SSR)...32
3. Market Value to Realized Value (MVRV).....................33
4. Miners Position Index (MPI)...33
5. Net Unrealized Profit/Loss (NUPL)...............................33

Fail-proof Indicator
What is the Pi Cycle Indicator?..34
How Is the Pi Cycle Top Indicator Calculated?................34
Does the Pi Cycle Top Indicator Really Work?................36

Conclusion..37

How to Identify the TOP of the crypto market

Bitcoin reached its historic high, Ether surpassed the U$ 4,891.00 barrier and the market as a whole is experiencing a strong rise, which will intensify even further with the 2024 Halving. Given this, many investors are already making significant profits and are questioning themselves: Whether they should be partially carried out?

Obviously we cannot predict short-term movements such as the intensity of corrections in these recent movements, but that is not the objective here. What we seek in this book is to observe the current moment from a medium long term perspective and compare it with past market cycles, in order to extract some valuable insights. The indicators that we will bring below have proven effective in signaling moments of extreme euphoria, and I can already say that they indicate that currently (March 2024) we are still far from a peak.

Bitcoin's dominance

The recent upward movement proved to be more advantageous for Bitcoin holders, as the asset performed much better than the crypto market average. Since November 2022, the bottom of the last bear market, Bitcoin's dominance over the crypto market as a whole has jumped from 40% to 55%, a movement characteristic of the first phase of a bullish cycle. The tendency is that until the peak of the cycle's euphoria, projected for mid-2025, this dominance will fall again and the financial flow will migrate to other assets, starting with ETH, then to more consolidated altcoins and finally to low capitalization coins. and memecoins.

The 4 Phases of a Market Cycle

Cycles are prevalent in all aspects of life; they range from the very short-term, like the life cycle of a June bug, which lives only a few days, to the life cycle of a planet, which takes billions of years. No matter what market you are referring to, all go through the same phases and are cyclical. They rise, peak, dip, and then bottom out. When one market cycle is finished, the next one begins.

The problem is that most investors and traders either fail to recognize that markets are cyclical or forget to expect the end of the current market phase. Another significant challenge is that even when you accept the existence of cycles, it is nearly impossible to pick the top or bottom of one. But an understanding of cycles is essential if you want to maximize investment or trading returns. Here are the four major components of a market cycle and how you can recognize them.

1. Accumulation Phase

This phase occurs after the market has bottomed and the innovators (corporate insiders and a few value investors) and early adopters (smart money managers and experienced traders) begin to buy, figuring the worst is over. At this phase, valuations are very attractive, and general market sentiment is still bearish.

Articles in the media preach doom and gloom, and those who were long through the worst of the bear market have recently given up and sold the rest of their holdings in disgust. However, in the accumulation phase, prices have flattened and for every seller throwing in the towel, someone is there to pick it up at a healthy discount. Overall market sentiment begins to switch from negative to neutral.

The 4 Phases of a Market Cycle

2. Mark-Up Phase

At this stage, the market has been stable for a while and is beginning to move higher. The early majority are getting on the bandwagon. This group includes technicians who, seeing the market is putting in higher lows and higher highs, recognize market direction and sentiment have changed.

Media stories begin to discuss the possibility that the worst is over, but unemployment continues to rise, as do reports of layoffs in many sectors. As this phase matures, more investors jump on the bandwagon as fear of being in the market is supplanted by greed and the fear of being left out.

As this phase begins to come to an end, the late majority jump in and market volumes begin to increase substantially. At this point, the greater fool theory prevails. Valuations climb well beyond historic norms, and logic and reason take a back seat to greed. While the late majority are getting in, the smart money and insiders are unloading.

But as prices begin to level off, or as the rise slows down, those laggards who have been sitting on the sidelines see this as a buying opportunity and jump in en masse. Prices make one last parabolic move, known in technical analysis as a selling climax when the largest gains in the shortest periods often happen. But the cycle is nearing the top. Sentiment moves from neutral to bullish to downright euphoric during this phase.

The 4 Phases of a Market Cycle

3. Distribution Phase

In the third phase of the market cycle, sellers begin to dominate. This part of the cycle is identified by a period in which the bullish sentiment of the previous phase turns into a mixed sentiment. Prices can often stay locked in a trading range that can last a few weeks or even months.

For example, when the Dow Jones Industrial Average (DJIA) peaked in Feb. 2020, it traded down to the vicinity of its prior peak and stayed there over a period of several months. But the distribution phase can come and go quickly. For the Nasdaq Composite, the distribution phase was less than a month long, as it peaked in Feb. 2020 and moved higher shortly thereafter. When this phase is over, the market reverses direction. Classic patterns like double and triple tops, as well as head and shoulders patterns, are examples of movements that occur during the distribution phase.

The distribution phase is a very emotional time for the markets, as investors are gripped by periods of complete fear interspersed with hope and even greed as the market may at times appear to be taking off again. Valuations are extreme in many issues and value investors have long been sitting on the sidelines. Usually, sentiment slowly but surely begins to change, but this transition can happen quickly if accelerated by a strongly negative geopolitical event or extremely bad economic news.

Those who are unable to sell for a profit settle for a breakeven price or a small loss.

The 4 Phases of a Market Cycle

4. Mark-Down Phase

The fourth and final phase in the cycle is the most painful for those who still hold positions. Many hang on because their investment has fallen below what they paid for it, behaving like the pirate who falls overboard clutching a bar of gold, refusing to let go in the vain hope of being rescued. It is only when the market has plunged 50% or more than the laggards, many of whom bought during the distribution or early markdown phase, give up or capitulate.

Unfortunately, this is a buy signal for early innovators and a sign that a bottom is imminent. But alas, it is new investors who will buy the depreciated investment during the next accumulation phase and enjoy the next mark-up.

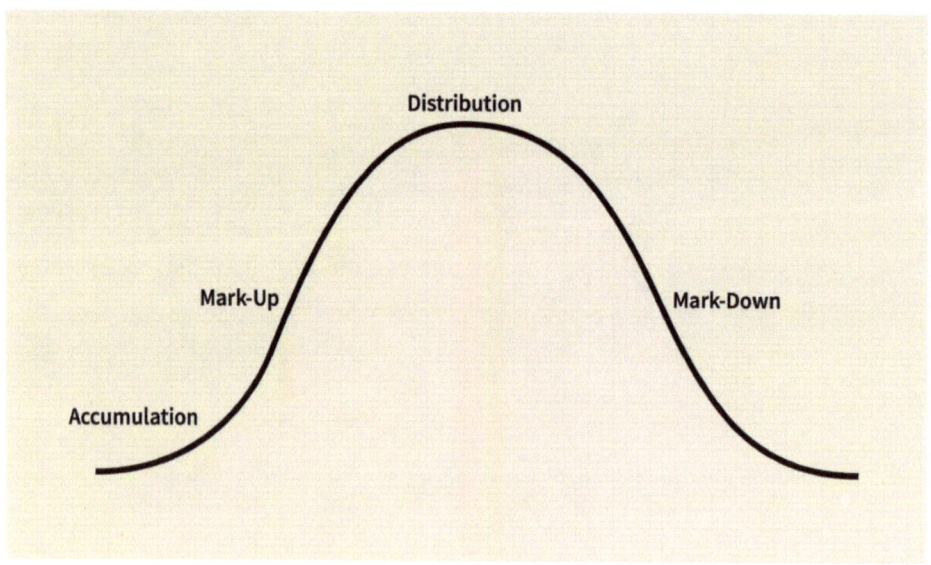

Crypto Money Flow Simplified

Crypto market cycles can also be viewed in a more simplified way, as shown in the graph below, which shows how the flow of money operates within the phases of the bullish cycle.

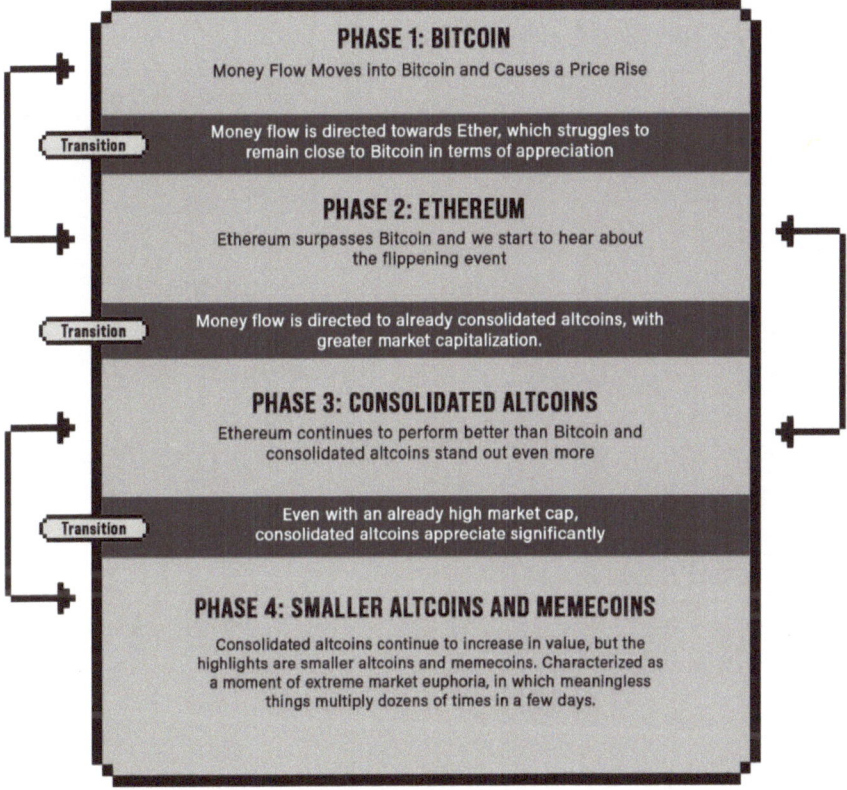

This movement has been noticeable in past cycles and this moment of attention rotation, which should occur during 2024, has proven to be a great time to take more risk in altcoins to the detriment of positions in BTC.

Altcoins Market Share

In the following graph, prepared by Pantera Capital, one of the most renowned Venture Capital funds on the market, we can observe the two main phases of a bull market: the moment in which Bitcoin appreciates more than the market average and increases its dominance and the moment when investors' attention turns mainly to altcoins, causing their performance to be superior.

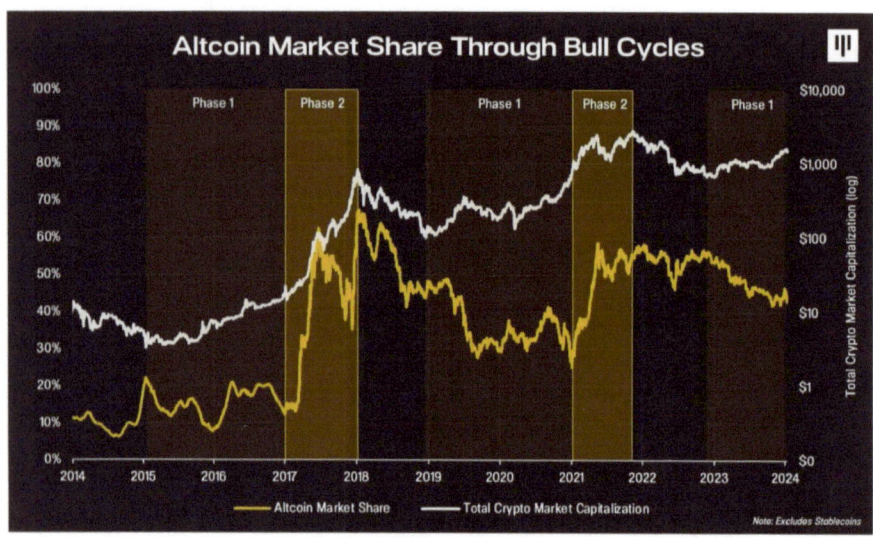

In these cycles, bitcoin consistently outperformed altcoins in phase 1 of the upswing. In phase 2, altcoins substantially outperformed bitcoin. What's interesting is that the magnitude of outperformance is so large that altcoins have outperformed bitcoin across the full length of both cycles. While one of the highest sources of alpha has historically come from a perfectly timed rotation from bitcoin into altcoins as phase 2 commences, that relationship won't necessarily always hold true nor is timing that rotation perfectly a reality for any trader. Perhaps the most feasible way to generate alpha in the space is by maintaining consistent exposure, investing in altcoins that have fundamental reasons to appreciate multiples more than bitcoin in total.

The Bitcoin Halving

What is Bitcoin Halving?

The Bitcoin Halving is when Bitcoin's mining reward is split in half. It takes the blockchain network about four years to open 210,000 more blocks, a standard set by the blockchain's creators to continuously reduce the rate at which the cryptocurrency is introduced.

The first reward was 50 bitcoin. Previous halving dates were:
- Nov. 28, 2012, to 25 bitcoins
- July 9, 2016, to 12.5 bitcoins
- May 11, 2020, to 6.25 bitcoins

The next halving is expected to occur in April 2024, when the block reward will fall to 3.125 BTC. As of March 2024, about 19.65 million bitcoins were in circulation, leaving just around 1.35 million to be released via mining rewards.

Basics of the Bitcoin Network

To understand a Bitcoin halving, you must first know how the Bitcoin network operates. Bitcoin's underlying technology, blockchain, consists of a network of computers (called nodes) that run Bitcoin's software and contain a partial or complete history of transactions occurring on its network. Each full node contains the entire history of transactions on Bitcoin and is responsible for approving or rejecting a transaction in Bitcoin's network. To do that, the node conducts a check to ensure the transaction is valid. These include ensuring the transaction contains the correct validation parameters and does not exceed the required length.

Each transaction is approved individually. This is said to occur only after all the transactions contained in a block are approved. After approval, the transaction is appended to the existing blockchain and broadcast to other nodes.

What is Bitcoin Halving?

Adding more computers (or nodes) to the blockchain increases its stability and security. There were 18,830 nodes estimated to be running Bitcoin's code on March 5, 2024. Although anyone can participate in Bitcoin's network as a node as long as they have enough storage to download the entire blockchain and its history of transactions, not all of them are miners.

Basics of Bitcoin Mining

Bitcoin mining is the process by which people use computers or mining hardware to participate in Bitcoin's blockchain network as transaction processors and validators. Miners receive rewards and transaction fees. Bitcoin uses a system called proof-of-work (PoW) to validate transaction information. It's called proof-of-work because solving the cryptographic puzzle takes time and energy, which acts as proof that work was done.

The term mining is not used literally but as a reference to how precious metals are harvested. When a block is filled with transactions, it is closed and sent to a mining queue. Once it is queued up for verification, Bitcoin miners compete to be the first to find a number with a value less than that of a target set by the network. The hash is a hexadecimal number that contains all of the encrypted information of the previous blocks.

Mining confirms the legitimacy of the transactions in a block and opens a new one. Nodes then verify the transactions further in a series of confirmations. This process creates a chain of blocks containing information, forming the blockchain.

BITCOIN HALVING EFFECTS

Bitcoin Halving Effects

Inflation

One of the key concepts behind halving the reward is to address inflation concerns. Inflation is a decrease in the amount of goods a certain amount of currency can buy at any given moment. In the U.S., inflation is measured by how much it costs to buy a basket of goods. There is an acceptable inflation rate that is considered good for an economy—usually 2%—but this number is generally a target set by central banks as a goal rather than a reachable figure.

The Bitcoin Halving is intended to counter any inflationary effects on Bitcoin by lowering the reward amount and maintaining scarcity. However, this inflation "protection" mechanism does not protect Bitcoin users from the inflationary effects of the fiat currency to which it must be converted to be used in an economy. Gains made regarding market value might offer inflation protection for investors, but it doesn't for the cryptocurrency's intended use as a payment method.

Investing

Bitcoin wasn't intended to be an investment. It was introduced as a payment method that attempted to remove the need to have regulatory agencies or third parties involved in transactions.

It became popular with investors once it was noted that there was the potential for gains. Investors poured into the new asset space, creating demand that the cryptocurrency's designers may not have anticipated. For investors, a halving represents a reduction in the new coin supply, but it also offers the promise of an increase in investment value if the event's effects remain the same. But this places Bitcoin investing into the realm of speculation because those invested in the cryptocurrency are hoping for gains.

Bitcoin Halving Effects

Demand

Because a halving reduces the number of new Bitcoins introduced, demand for new Bitcoins generally increases. This can be noted by looking at Bitcoin's price after each previous halving event—it has generally risen.

Mining

Miners are the people, groups, or businesses that focus on mining for its profitability. When new Bitcoins are awarded, the miner(s) that receive the reward have been making substantial gains in the past. As Bitcoin's price fluctuated over the years, it remained a lucrative endeavor—if it hadn't, the large mining businesses wouldn't have continued operating.

However, a halving cuts mining rewards, so the endeavor becomes less profitable with each halving if prices remain the same or drop. The large-scale mining facilities needed to remain competitive require enormous amounts of money and energy. The equipment and facilities need maintenance and people to conduct it. They also need to upgrade their mining capacity to maintain their position in the industry.

For instance, Marathon Digital Holdings, one of the world's largest mining firms, increased its Bitcoin holdings to 16,930 and its fleet of Bitcoin miners to 231,000 in February 2024. This brings the firm's hash rate to 28.7 trillion hashes per second (5% of the network's total hash rate as of March 5, 2024). The increase in production capacity and holdings was likely due to anticipations of the next halving and the amount of hashing power required to remain competitive while having the liquidity necessary to finance its operations.

For smaller miners, a decrease in the reward means lower chances. Miners who are part of a mining pool will likely experience smaller rewards, even if prices increase—the reward is being cut in half, but Bitcoin's price is not likely to double to maintain current profitability unless there is a drastic market event.

Bitcoin Halving Effects

Consumers

Consumers and retail Bitcoin users might be affected by a halving in the value of the Bitcoin they hold. Those who buy Bitcoin for making purchases will generally only be affected by price fluctuations, which may or may not remain similar to those before the halving occurred.

For those using Bitcoin for remittances, a halving means the same thing as it does for shoppers. The value of their remittances will depend on Bitcoin's market price after the halving event.

What Happens When Bitcoin Halves?

The term "halving" as it relates to Bitcoin concerns how many tokens are rewarded. This acts as a way to simulate diminishing returns, theoretically intended to raise demand. The Bitcoin mining algorithm is set with a target of finding new blocks once every 10 minutes. Some blocks take more than 10 minutes; some take less. This can decrease or increase the amount of time it takes to reach the next halving goal. For example, if blocks consecutively average 9.66 minutes to mine, it would take about 1,409 days to mine the 210,000 blocks required (four years is 1461 days, including one day for a leap year).

What Happens When There Are No More Bitcoins Left?

It is often thought that in 2140, the last bitcoin will be mined. However, if the reward is halved every 210,000 blocks, it will get smaller and smaller until one satoshi is the reward and the total amount circulating equals 21 million. One satoshi is 0.00000001 bitcoin—it is the lowest denomination of Bitcoin and cannot be halved.

Bitcoin Halving Effects

The Bottom Line

A Bitcoin halving cuts the rate at which new Bitcoins are released into circulation in half. The rewards system is expected to continue until the year 2140 when the proposed limit of 21 million bitcoin is theoretically reached.

In 2009, the reward for each block in the chain mined was 50 bitcoins. After the first halving, it was 25, and then 12.5, and then it became 6.25 bitcoins per block as of May 11, 2020. It's expected to halve again in April 2024.

Bitcoin halving has major implications for its network. For miners, the halving event may result in consolidation in their ranks as individual miners and small outfits drop out of the mining ecosystem or are taken over by larger players.

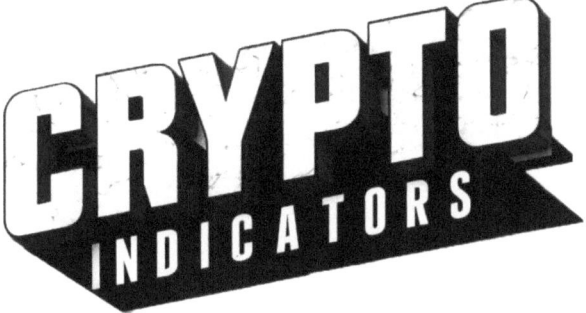

Social Sentiment Indicators

Social sentiment indicators can be quantitative or qualitative. To pick a social sentiment indicator that best fits your analysis, you can first decide what kind of information is valuable to you — the popularity of a search term, the sentiment, or both. The absolute popularity gives you valuable information of the aggregated social attraction on various platforms. The relative popularity records the speed or the share of social attraction of a search term. The sentiment indicators quantify and categorize people's moods towards a search term, for example, positive or negative, greedy or fear.

Social indicators reveal the level of engagement of retail investors with the crypto market. If we compare current metrics with those from the peak of the last bull, in the second half of 2021, we see that we are still a long way from a top of attention. We can access interesting social indicators in The Block's alternative metrics category and on Google Trends by entering terms like "Crypto" and "Bitcoin" in the search field.

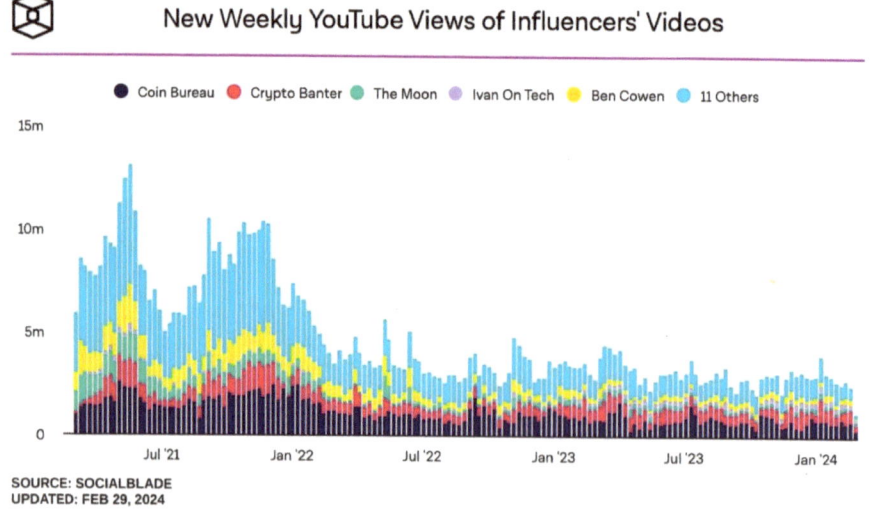

Social Sentiment Indicators

Google searches for the term "Crypto"

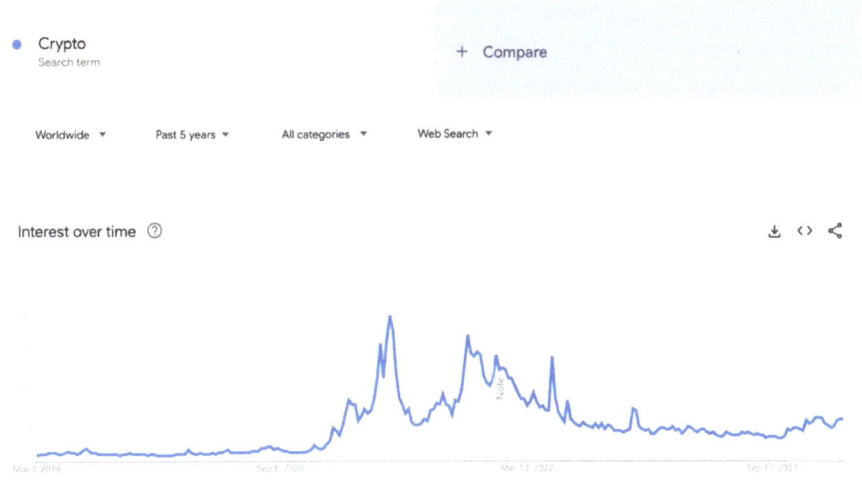

Another interesting social indicator to be analyzed is the download ranking of the biggest cryptocurrency brokerage apps. Crypto exchange Coinbase has surged back into the U.S. Apple App Store top 100 for the first time in more than two years. The app jumped from a ranking of 163rd on Sunday to 98th yesterday as the price of bitcoin approached all-time highs. It has since leaped back into the top 50 — currently ranking at 49th — according to The Block's data dashboard.

On-chain metrics

On-chain analysis is a fundamental resource for understanding market momentum. Indicators such as MVRV have proven to be an essential tool for conscious decision-making in moments of extreme euphoria and extreme fear. MVRV (Market Value to Realized Value) is an indicator used to visualize whether Bitcoin holders' portfolios have unrealized profits or losses, as well as to what extent. The lower the indicator, the more portfolios are at unrealized loss.

Normally, only highly convinced and long-term-thinking investors hold the asset when the indicator is close to its minimum level. The higher the indicator, the more portfolios are in profit. Typically, long-term investors take the opportunity to take profits when the indicator is close to its maximum level. In the following graph, we can highlight two regions. The region below 1 represents a loss for holders, the moment in which the market price is below the average acquisition price of investors. This is typical of late-stage bear markets and is often associated with bottoming and accumulation. The region above 1 represents the moment in which holders are making profits, so that the higher the number, the greater the intensity of these profits and the greater the propensity to realize profits. Historically, values greater than 3.0 have signaled overheated bull markets. Although we have already left the best accumulation zone, we are still relatively far from an overheated market scenario.

On-chain metrics - MRVR Z-Score

The indicators mentioned above show us that the peak of maximum euphoria in the market is still missing. Over the next 12 to 18 months, this movement tends to evolve even further and anyone who knows how to position themselves well will now be able to take advantage of the opportunities, even with the normal fluctuations in the crypto market.

The Z-Score is one of the best metrics for knowing the best time to buy and sell Bitcoin. Simple, in the green areas we have the bottoms, the best times to buy, while in the red areas we have the market peaks, the best times to sell. Note that we are beginning an upward curve in the Z-Score, with a large margin of accumulation until we reach the red area again. We need to take into account that in the Bear Market, it can always fall more and in the Bull Market, it can always rise more, it is a science still under construction.

On-Chain Analysis: An In-Depth Look

The MVRV Z-Score chart that I presented on previous pages is just one of the on-chain analysis possibilities available for the crypto market. I invite you to take a deeper dive into discovering this tool that can be a game changer for an exponential profit in your portfolio, and will give you increasingly clear and assertive notions about the best time to buy or exit a cryptocurrency, especially those Altcoins.

The cryptocurrency revolution has brought with it not only new ways of transferring value, but also a vast amount of data that is immutably recorded on blockchains. This data, publicly available for anyone to examine, forms the basis of on-chain analytics - an essential approach to understanding the workings and trends of cryptocurrency ecosystems.

1. What is On-Chain Analysis

On-chain analysis involves exploring and interpreting data that is recorded on cryptocurrency blockchains. Unlike technical analysis that focuses on price patterns and fundamental analysis that focuses on the economic and technological aspects of currencies, on-chain analysis is based on the raw transaction data, wallet addresses, and smart contracts present on blockchains.

Blockchains are like large public ledgers and decentralized systems that record all transactions and interactions on the network. Each transaction is a permanent record of value transferring between different wallet addresses. By analyzing these records, we can gain insights into how coins are being moved, who is carrying out the transactions and what are the behavior patterns of network participants.

On-Chain Analysis: An In-Depth Look

2. Definition and Context

On-chain analysis is facilitated by blockchin explorers, online platforms that allow users to search and examine transactions, addresses and smart contracts. These tools provide graphs and metrics that help you understand network dynamics. The immutability of on-chain data is a fundamental pillar, ensuring that information cannot be changed retroactively.

3. The On-Chain Analysis difference

While technical analysis and fundamental analysis focus mainly in price patterns, economic indicators and market events, on-chain analysis is based on objective data registered on blockchains. This approach differs from others in its focus on the tangible reality of transactions and activities on the network, making it a powerful tool for understanding the real dynamics of the cryptocurrency ecosystem, regardless of price fluctuations or market sentiments.

In a simple way, through on-chain data it is possible to analyze, make decisions and substantiate theories with data that, in the private environment, are non-existent or completely private. Evaluating real-time behavior of large investors, measuring current losses of specific addresses and measuring flows are some of the types of tangible approaches in this sector, in a tool made possible through the transparency of blockchain technology, providing a great advantage for investors who know whether use this data.

On-Chain Analysis: Tools and resources

1. Understanding the origin of data

On-chain analysis requires understanding key elements registered on blockchains. Transactions are records of value transfer between wallet addresses. Each transaction has information such as sender, recipient and amount transferred. Wallet addresses are unique identifiers associated with network participants. Furthermore, smart contracts are autonomous programs that automatically perform actions when certain conditions are met.

2. Identifying patterns and insights

On-chain analysis transcends mere data observation, seeking intrinsic patterns to gain deeper understandings. By exploring data recorded on blockchains, it is possible to identify patterns that reveal significant trends and behaviors of network participants. This identification of patterns is essential for predicting future movements and making informed decisions in the cryptocurrency ecosystem.

Transaction Volume Patterns:
Looking at transaction volumes over time can reveal moments of high activity, often associated with important events, project launches or crucial announcements. Patterns of sudden or gradual increases in volume may suggest impending volatility or potential trend reversals.

On-Chain Analysis: Tools and resources

Exchange Input and Output Flows:

Analyzing currency flows between personal wallets and exchanges can provide crucial insights into investor intent. Large volumes entering exchanges may indicate preparations for trading or selling, while exits may signal times of profit taking. Understanding these flows helps you anticipate buying or selling pressures.

Accumulation and Distribution:

Through on-chain analysis, it is possible to detect periods of accumulation, where investors are purchasing coins at low prices in anticipation of future highs, and periods of distribution, where they are selling at higher prices to realize profits. Observing the movement patterns of large amounts of currencies allows you to identify holders' intentions and possible changes in direction in the market.

Five On-Chain Indicators

1. Stock-to-Flow (S2F)

The Stock-to-Flow (S2F) indicator is a metric that relates the total amount of a cryptocurrency in circulation (stock) with the newly mined quantity (flow). Generally applied to Bitcoin, the S2F is used to assess scarcity and future availability of a cryptocurrency. The higher the S2F value, the greater the relative scarcity, the which can positively influence appreciation over time.

This model treats Bitcoin as being comparable to commodities such as gold, silver or platinum. These are known as 'store of value' commodities because they retain value over long time frames due to their relative scarcity. It is difficult to significantly increase their supply i.e. the process of searching for gold and then mining it is expensive and takes time. Bitcoin is similar because it is also scarce. In fact, it is the first-ever scarce digital object to exist. There are a limited number of coins in existence and it will take a lot of electricity and computing effort to mine the 3 million outstanding coins still to be mined, therefore the supply rate is consistently low. Stock-to-flow ratios are used to evaluate the current stock of a commodity (total amount currently available) against the flow of new production (amount mined that specific year)

Five On-Chain Indicators

1. Stock-to-Flow (S2F) - HOW TO VIEW THE CHART

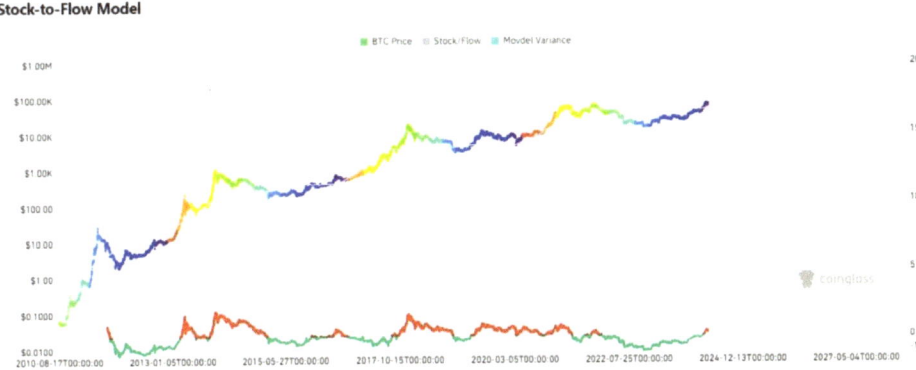

On the above chart price is overlaid on top of the stock-to-flow ratio line. We can see that price has continued to follow the stock-to-flow of Bitcoin over time. The theory, therefore, suggests that we can project where price may go by observing the projected stock-to-flow line, which can be calculated as we know the approximate mining schedule of future Bitcoin mining. The coloured dots on the price line of this chart show the number of days until the next Bitcoin halving (sometimes called 'halvening') event. This is an event where the reward for mining new blocks is halved, meaning miners receive 50% fewer bitcoins for verifying transactions. Bitcoin halvings are scheduled to occur every 210,000 blocks – roughly every four years – until the maximum supply of 21 million bitcoins has been generated by the network. That makes stock-to-flow ratio (scarcity) higher so in theory price should go up. This has held true previously in Bitcoin's history. The stock-to-flow line on this chart incorporates a 365-day average into the model to smooth out the changes caused in the market by the halving events. In addition to the main stock-to-flow chart, I have created a divergence chart (lower section of the chart) which shows the difference between price and stock-to-flow. When price moves above stock-to-flow (divergence line turns from green to red), thereby allowing us to easily see how price interacts with stock-to-flow through market cycles over time.

Five On-Chain Indicators

2. Stablecoin Supply Ratio (SSR)

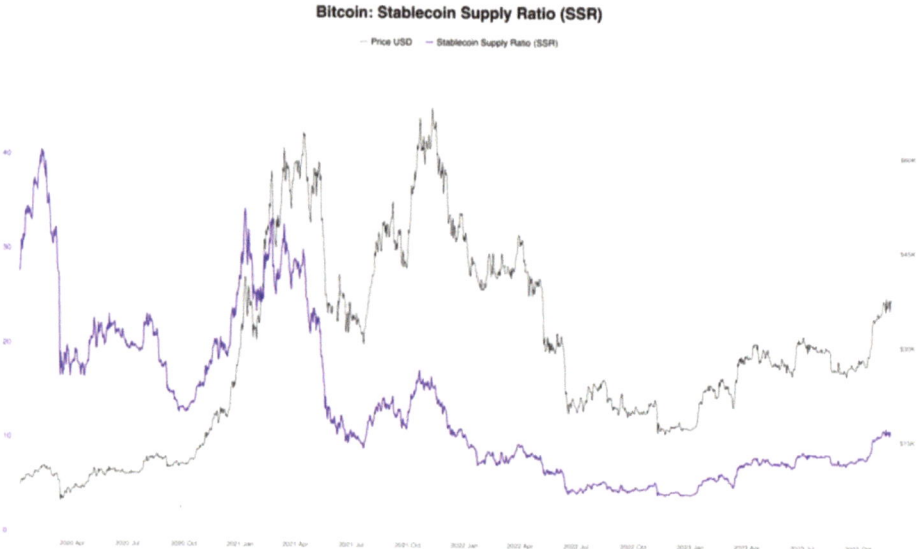

    The Stablecoin Supply Ratio (SSR) indicator evaluates the relationship between the total supply of stablecoins, which are cryptocurrencies anchored to fiat currencies such as the dollar, and the total capitalization of the cryptocurrency market. The SSR is used to identify liquidity ready to enter the market. An increase in SSR suggests greater buying capacity, while a decrease may indicate that investors are more likely to sell.

    A Stablecoin Supply Ratio (SSR) of 5 indicates that the market cap of Bitcoin is five times larger than the combined market cap of all stablecoins. Traders might interpret this as a time when Bitcoin holds a dominant position, and stablecoins are relatively less in demand. Conversely, if the SSR were, for instance, 0.2, it would signify a situation where the market capitalization of stablecoins is five times larger than that of Bitcoin. This could imply high potential buying pressure on stablecoins, supporting a possible value rise.

Five On-Chain Indicators

3. Market Value to Realized Value (MVRV)

As we have seen in the book previously, but we could not help but remember, the Market Value to Realized Value (MVRV) indicator compares the current market value of a cryptocurrency with its realized value. The realized value is calculated based on the price at the time the coins were last moved. A high MVRV can indicate possible overvaluation, suggesting caution, while a low MVRV can indicate undervaluation and possible buying opportunities.

4. Miners Position Index (MPI)

The Miners Position Index (MPI) is an indicator that tracks the behavior of cryptocurrency miners. It reveals whether the Miners are hoarding or selling their newly mined rewards. An increase in MPI may suggest mining companies are optimistic about future prices, while a decrease may indicate the opposite. MPI offers unique insights into mining companies' outlook on the market.

5. Net Unrealized Profit/Loss (NUPL)

The Net Unrealized Profit/Loss (NUPL) indicator evaluates the profit or loss of coin holders at the time the coins were moved. A high NUPL suggests that many holders are taking profits, indicating a possible market correction. On the other hand, a low NUPL could indicate that holders are at a loss, which could signal buying opportunities.

Fail-proof Indicator

To close this topic with a flourish, we bring you an indicator that has never failed since it was created: **Pi Cycle Top**

The Pi Cycle Top Indicator has managed to predict Bitcoin bull market cycle tops with ridiculous accuracy in the past. So what is this indicator, how does it work, and can we use it to our advantage? Let's dive in!

What is the Pi Cycle Indicator?

The Pi Cycle Top Indicator is an incredibly simple, but effective combination of technical indicators. Even though the strategy is based merely on a combination of two moving averages, it has managed to predict four different cycle tops with amazing accuracy. With this track record, many Bitcoin investors look to the Pi Cycle Top Indicator to predict the next Bitcoin market cycle high. First published by LookIntoBitcoin founder, Philip Swift, the Pi Cycle Top indicator can be found in the toolbox of many Bitcoin investors. But how does it work?

How Is the Pi Cycle Top Indicator Calculated?

To generate Pi Cycle Top signals, Philip Swift put together a combination of two daily moving averages: the 111-day moving average and a 2x multiplication of the 350-day moving average. Both moving averages are long-term indicators, but the 111-day moving average is more responsive to price than its 350-day counterpart, as it uses far fewer days to compute an average.

Fail-proof Indicator

Under normal conditions, the 2x multiplication of a 350-day moving average should be far above the 111-day moving average – and for most of Bitcoin history, it has. The rare moments, where that 111-day moving average crosses above its multiplied 350-day counterpart, trigger the Pi Cycle Top signal.

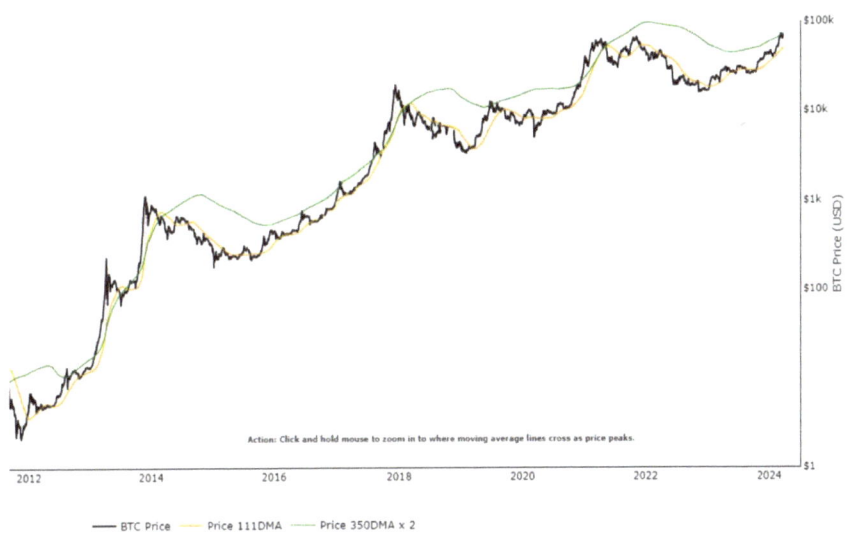

In the image above, the yellow line indicates a 111-day moving average. **Whenever it crossed above the 350-day average (green line) even if briefly, the market marked the cycle top**. Looking back, that signal has been an accurate indicator of Bitcoin cycle highs. Has your question about the top of the market been answered?

Fun Fact: When you divide 350 by 111, is 3.153 – really close to the mathematical Pi number (3.142). What a name, right?

Fail-proof Indicator

Does the Pi Cycle Top Indicator Really Work?

As discussed, the Pi Cycle Top Indicator has managed to accurately time the top of the previous market cycles. However, it is worth noting that the indicator was designed only in April of 2019, which is after the first three signals took place.

Only the most recent signal was printed after the indicator was published, and Bitcoin still managed to push higher after that, although the market did pull back over 50% following the signal. Critics argue the model has been curve-fitted, and that the most recent signal coinciding with the market top is a coincidence. At this point, it is hard to tell if they are right or not – a new market cycle will have to find its highs before we'll know for sure.

All in all, the Pi Cycle Top Indicator is an interesting indicator to observe, but it needs time to prove its worth. As with any indicator, it is unwise to base trading decisions purely on the signals provided by that indicator. Instead, perform your analysis with multiple tools, and act on those conclusions when they are aligned.

Conclusion

In this book we had the opportunity to better understand Cryptocurrency Market Cycles, the main tools for analyzing market trends and also the meaning of Halving for Bitcoin and the market as a whole.

Now my question is: **With this knowledge, can you answer more precisely, when is the best time to sell your Bitcoins, or rather, your cryptocurrencies?**

I speak about cryptocurrencies in a generic way, as my investor profile is long-term. I see Bitcoin as a deflationary, scarce currency with constant and everlasting growth, so I don't think about selling it anytime soon, it's my self-custodied private pension.

It's not easy to answer this question, even for traditional investments: experts often differ in opinions about when would be the most appropriate time to get rid of a share, when it's best to get rid of a public security, when you should sell an option. With Bitcoin the scenario is even more difficult: as it is a cryptocurrency and, therefore, belonging to an asset class that is still very new (only ten years old), the pricing and valuation models are still being discovered and tested, without that there is a consensus on what would be the most appropriate methods to identify the best moments of entry or exit.

Without having a consolidated valuation method, what seems to work best to identify tops and bottoms is the chart, the good old on-chain analysis. Mastering on-chain analysis does not require support from hidden forces, but rather a lot of study, time, dedication and practice. There are many indicators and, to be successful in a trade, you need to know how they work and how they usually behave.

Conclusion

And it's not enough to just master on-chain analysis: you need to have time every day to analyze the chart, as trends and indicators change all the time. Does this mean that we, mere mortals, who are not great graphics artists should be left to our luck to make good sales? No way. As I said, Bitcoin pricing and valuation models are still being developed and tested, but in its brief history we already have some indicators with a good track record of predictive capacity.

Among the indicators presented in the book, the most assertive are the MVRV and the PI CYCLE TOP, which has never failed! Of course, indicators always have distortions, as they interpret every movement as a purchase and sale of bitcoins, but this does not mean that they cannot be useful. If we historically analyze the correlation between the price and the MVRV, we will see that the indicator was able to identify several moments when Bitcoin was overvalued and moments when it was undervalued, including the big drop in 2018 and the bottom found in December. Historically, an MVRV below 1 indicates Bitcoin is undervalued, while an MVRV above 4 indicates overvalued. Currently (March 2024) the MVRV is above level 2, indicating the beginning of an upward trajectory until reaching levels above 7, in the sales region.

It is true that both indicators have an excellent track record for finding Bitcoin tops, but this may mean absolutely nothing. Why? Because if the hypothesis of efficient markets (which gave Eugene Fama the Nobel Prize in economics) is correct, economic agents assimilate all available information and price assets accordingly, anticipating future movements. In this way, the above indicators would have already been verified and priced, having little or no use for the investor. I am a staunch supporter of the efficient markets hypothesis, even for the cryptocurrency market. So, what is the proper way to know when you should sell your bitcoins?

Conclusion

In the end, it's quite simple: **have goals**. It doesn't matter what they are: it could be buying a car, having an appreciation of x% or having a target price of y dollars. Once your goal is reached, sell. You don't need to close your positions completely, but you can have percentage goals for achieving or even converting Altcoins into Bitcoin, if your goal is to accumulate bitcoins, regardless of the price.

We need to keep in mind that the prices defined by the market are established in the collective mind of investors who try to predict the future and the Great Whales, who try to manipulate the market, that is, nothing is 100% certain, as we are navigating in spheres that go beyond mathematics and are much closer to financial psychology and human behavior.

Using this strategy of partial goals and achievements, it is unlikely that you will sell for the best price, but the reality is that this does not matter. Investments are not ends in themselves, they are not a race: it doesn't matter who gets there faster or further, the important thing is that you get where you want to go. And today Bitcoin is one of the main means responsible for bringing investors closer and closer to their dreams. For many people, retirement and Bitcoin don't mix, but the numbers are proving that this theory is already obsolete. In fact, Bitcoin can even accelerate the achievement of major goals such as financial independence if used correctly.

I close this book with my sincere hope that the information compiled and presented here will make a difference in your life and the lives of many others, and that you will be able to achieve all your goals in turbo mode, driven by the magic that Halving can do with our capital .

.

www.ingramcontent.com/pod-product-compliance
Lightning Source LLC
Chambersburg PA
CBHW040336220526
45473CB00009B/2701